WEAPONS GRADE

ALSO BY TERESE SVOBODA

POETRY

All Aberration
Laughing Africa
Mere Mortals
Treason

FICTION

Cannibal
A Drink Called Paradise
Trailer Girl and Other Stories
Tin God

MEMOIR

Black Glasses Like Clark Kent

TRANSLATION

Cleaned The Crocodile's Teeth

WEAPONS GRADE

POEMS BY TERESE SVOBODA

The University of Arkansas Press

Fayetteville

2009

ISBN-10: 1-55728-906-9
ISBN-13: 978-1-55728-906-3

13   12   11   10   09   5   4   3   2   1

Designed by Liz Lester

⊛ The paper used in this publication meets the minimum requirements
of the American National Standard for Permanence of Paper for Printed
Library Materials Z39.48-1984.

LIBRARY OF CONGRESS CATALOGING-IN-PUBLICATION DATA

Svoboda, Terese.
        Weapons grade : poems / by Terese Svoboda.
            p.   cm.
        ISBN 978-1-55728-906-3 (pbk. : alk. paper)
        I. Title.
        PS3569.V6W43   2009
        811'.54—dc22
                                2009018536

To Eleanor Wilner,
with much love

ACKNOWLEDGMENTS

"Mom as Fly," *New Yorker;* "Aphra Plays," *Paris Review;* "Burnt House," *Tin House;* "My Mature Style," *Times Literary Supplement;* "Secret Executions of Black GIs in Occupied Japan," "To My Brother, on the Occasion of his Second Breakdown," and "The Dog in the Wall," *Ploughshares;* "Code Name: 731," "Carwreck," "Midwest Glacier," "Picnic Portents," and "Steam Seams," *Hotel Amerika;* "For They Know Not What They Do," "Wooly Bully," "A Bag, Moving Slightly, in Black and White," "Apprehend Us," and "An Old War," *American Poetry Review;* "The Convoy Never Moves," *Boston Review;* "Hurricane Girl" (part 1), *32 Poems;* "Hurricane Girl" (part 2) as "Scylla" and "Miss Givings" as "Disingenuous," *Qualm.com;* "Hurricane Girl" (part 3) as "Swollen Victory," "Hand Quest," and "Whose XLM," *Denver Quarterly;* "Pineal," "Love Light," and "Motion Makes Us Cough," *Blackbird;* "Motion Makes Us Cough," reprinted in *The Page;* "Flaw," *Tiferet;* "Cycles," *Cortland Review;* "Bicoastal" and "Two Groundhogs," *Mangrove;* "Sousa at Seventeen," *Witness;* "DeToq," *Drunken Boat;* "Slave Children," *Yale Review;* "Hamlet Hirsute," "Bad Neighbor" and "I Think of Pilgrims," *Guernica;* "Animal Lover," *Columbia;* "The Gift of Funny" and "Three Plucked Ladies" as "The Sun Burns," *Barrow Street;* "Sussurus of Sheets, Goodbye," *Agni;* "Stalled," *St. Petersburg Review;* "Jean/Jeanne Baret," *Degrees of Freedom;* "Alveoli," *Gulf Coast Review;* "Octopus," *Valparaiso Poetry Review;* "The Widow's Walk," *Tuesday: An Art Project;* "Vets," *Iowa Review.*

Very big thanks to the Writers Room, the Corporation of Yaddo, The Rockefeller Foundation Bellagio Center, Maureen Seaton, Stephanie Strickland, Mary Sherman Willis, Nell Altizer, Leslie Daniels, and Steve Bull. Special thanks to Enid Shomer for her careful ear and kind heart.

CONTENTS

IV

I

The King of France—is he as tall as I am?
—HENRY VIII

PICNIC PORTENTS

Spiders live in all the park cupolas,
                              the joints
              she ties the balloons to.

                    See the fake steer roping,
the wire horns and the stiff rope? It's this hollering that exhausts,
       not the horseshoes.

                    Fishing for forks, she says,
When my husband dies then I'll know.
Who said sex
              and death for seventy?
Jeopardy.

While parachuting down,
he pinned on stripes and medals—a corporal's—
              so they would treat him better. That one, over there—

              It was in the mayo. Thirteen out of forty,
       two infants. You'd think they would have choked
on the potato.

Danae puts the box with the boy and herself in
out
       past the boat launch.
              Someone says that child
will kill his grandfather.

THE CONVOY NEVER MOVES

*Why should we hear about body bags,
and deaths . . . I mean, it's not relevant.
Why should I waste my beautiful mind
on something like that?*

—BARBARA BUSH on ABC's
Good Morning America,
March 18, 2003

Flow—the guests take themselves in
and out of the utility room while
you dream them, flowing, always
backward-glancing, from the window
who would leave open with such weather
arriving with each of them? While

guests, not people you would live
with, guests not people you would
talk too much to, just *How can you
help me?* these guests are already
dead but you can't tell as they back out
of the back room with *love*

on their lips, but you can tell
if you look out that window
where the convoy never moves
yet tugs moan, moan again
in ecstasy, and the guests flow,
looking for other rooms, utility

4

being not useful to them really,
being dead already, and they move
back to where they are allowed,
into the cavities of your body while
you run in place because your mind
won't stir—the convoy never moves.

FOR THEY KNOW NOT
WHAT THEY DO

There are soldiers in mother's hair
and soldiers peeling the screen.
Distracted? I am driven.
I can't stop this chattering
with history hissing its heat.

Grave raincoat-shouldered people
with their own histories, bad
histories, drink to their bitterness
and chide us for our efforts.
What is there other than *I forget?*

I can't read the papers, or your face
on the phone. *Give it up* is the answer, *is*
is the answer, *aghast* is the hair.
The rain's washed off most of our skin.
How does it feel during a war?

A silence stirs.

OCCUPATION

What do you do?
I try to occupy myself.

Resistance fighters resist,
not insurgents
who just want to live
where they live.

✖

We are occupied
(as in port-a-potty)
by p.r. No one cries
censored—or shitty.

✖

Truman's good idea explodes
in their irises. On the road
to Tokyo, they turn their faces
away from our jeeps. To erase us?

✖

The Spanish in Ireland:
my mother's black hair.
It's hand-to-hand,
rape even the mare.

✖

Bless me father for I have sinned.
The chaplain says it's in the wind.
Go home now. It's all right.
Let them at that last rewrite.

SECRET EXECUTIONS OF BLACK GIs
IN OCCUPIED JAPAN

Is the sleeve of that racist century
as wrought or gold-chained
        as Henry VIII's who strolls in and says
            I'm what matters,
                    intestines sagging, the regal spittle

bound to stick on dog fur? That's where the baby
finds it later. *Ah-blue-gabe.*
            Little Henry can't explain;
he has a lisp
the present masks.

The world yesterday, its white shoes at the paper door

        —I mean the MP's white gloves of innocence—

no mud in and no one steals
a giant MP's shoes
just the geisha drugs herself into another tenderness
where, a half century on,
            Mt. Rushmore
will rise in one-third size
in concrete.

        The MPs arrest (memory)
a whole country

when few knew
mushroom *bloom*
to outstrip the lilac.
     Our soldiers sat in
Zeroes after,
    hidden in long rows
under
cherry trees.

    I don't remember that, my uncle says.
All those months move together so many years
     gone: the red-furred dog he tamed,

his left-behind baby, the words—

Why did they do it?

a girl with bloody hands to lick,
the century unforgiven.
Jennifer, Jennifer—I can't read you—

O Kyochan, your long silk sleeve
brushing his brow—

and speech covering the synapse
with idiot noise
    which masks—

   Wait the zeroes converge the baby's O
mouth spread for egg
   the race soon enough testes-free
like the fast fading frog's.

O Mothra, so Mother, so monster,
your wings over the egg—

save us too.

　　　My uncle guarded the postwar's worst,
　　　　　　　　　　　worse after
　　　　　the military's who-do-you-think-you-are
　　　　　　　　　　　　　　　here
after the war is over—
　　　　　　　GIs kept
in twenty-foot holes dug
　　　into the frozen ground,
covered with sewer lids,
　　　　　or in sit-down cages, i.e.,
you can't stand up and you can't
sit down
　　　　　　　　for hours,
a prison where GI beat GI
(they could, not ought)
　　　and the winter lasted, nuclear or not,
　　　a naught no child could grasp,
nor the rah-rah recruits, their sleeves
　　　　　　　soon thick
　　　with insignia.

　　　　　MacArthur was God and King,
a man all capitals
with a face-mask as heavy
　　　as a Kwakiutl's,
someone you don't ever know enough of.

Born old in Little Rock,
               he used bayonets
        on retreating WWI vets camped beside the Capitol

in 1932.

In 1945
was worshipped,
        but not by Truman.

Black GIs jive marching one-two, one-and-a-two
Black GIs prodded by white MPs to—

Suicide is the option

for the too-old-to-remember
but first

a lot of ice   zeroes falling in big clumps

a screengame
                Weapons Grade

only the blood
               is so frozen, a stick of blood
you have to wedge
in before
time's up

        where oil spews,
        palms flare.

Will the MPs
who took those pictures, e.g., an iced
person of color
bashed bruised wrapped in plastic,
kill themselves?

Sick of blood, the white gloves,
the shoes
tracking it in, the dog tracking
tenderness, the paper door—there's
the drug—blackness.

Mind the car,
its vanishing, a Toyota built
out of war
driven to suicide.
The flicker.
The Flickr. *Abu who?*

His captain had a gallows
built by Japanese carpenters.
Even Korean vets spoke of it.
No Tyburn Tree,
where King Henry's 70,000 hanged but
American.

Fluorescence de jour,
a white light guiding (not the black to dance to)
on not off on not off
the rope coiled in an *O* that says

Say Can You See? what the century
is made of.

> Just placeholders,
> Suzie Wong's nipples. GIs.

Arrest those overwrought.
No one else remembers when all the zeroes were
nooses, all the ones stepped up.

We wear the mask of the guy who did it—

the present.

CODE NAME: 731

In the '90s 731's doctor ran the Japanese lab that
distributed AIDS-laden blood for transfusions.

                    The Tokyo developer's
Let there be land! unearths one cell of 731,
the Asian Auschwitz
          where
                    live GIs lost their livers
          to the Japanese whitecoats. A dragon steps forward in
big flame, mushroom smoke and
                    add to this, fawning. Stomach talk: U.S. and
                    Tokyo. Weeds

                                                  occupy
the world. Is there sense to that?

To yet meet the field's dragons,
                    grief airs itself as joke.
                              The ballerina geisha
with only four toes a foot circles,
          a wee wee wee all the way home.

                    We were going to be in trouble if American
                    soldiers asked us about the specimens.

                    says the 84-year-old nurse Toyo Ishii
to *Japan Times,* September 10, 2006.

No time for fire.

Or so the nurse said, her name
        the same as the "Secret of Secrets"
director.

                        His hospital curls up,
vanishes under Toyama No. 5 apartment block.
        The geisha's toes go just over the bones,
the dragon's teeth waves its maimed warriors,
                        the field's so green and besides—
                        B-side of that tune—
the reptile egg hatches
in the dirt,
the mother pooping them then
                        webbing away into the PBS
                        ballerina-themed
        sunrise/set, flashing post-atomic fire,
all wind-up.

                        Because nothing stays buried,
(surely hyperbole, where doubt digs) sidereal time slips,

stomachs talk and now we feel all those dendrons,
sighting dragons, a big number—731—

                        citing lot
        and the footnotes of where the Japanese
        nurse worked,
no geisha, no ballerina but octogenarian who tells you
        your toes, your little held back giggle ready to launch
pigs big and little, none alien, all-American,

allowed no prosecution,
    which is how we bought their files.

    We bought the files.
                How much cold can a body take?
How little liver?
    The boys' bones turn up in the Tokyo lot.

MOTION MAKES US COUGH

Emotion is more electrical,
our foot caught on the cord,
the blink we have to take.

Don't explain, says the little bird.
Don't tell who we are either.
Up and down the tarmac

fly guns in crates like sausages,
links of what we think we need.
Not me, not me,

chirps the chirper. But
there we are, yelling again,
or crying, or frying—

blinking. Manmade
fritz lies behind
muscle and even brain.

Why, that smile,
while not shocking, belies
emotion's grounding: sic,

read as written, if we can,
with these dark plugs out.
We will still cough.

A LOG-LOCKED NATION

Nothing so national as a flag,
the man says. A pink or blue wound

you could take a pick to,
a little level ground with tainted water.

You could reconsider, the man says.
He puts up a wet finger. No fire set

today will burn that far in this wind.
Clouds of dust turn into clouds.

Meanwhile, the trees log
every escape effort,

the country serves itself,
the enemy questions its crouching.

SOUSA AT SEVENTEEN

After the joyful belch of lunch,
the band secures its bells,
its uniforms stiff
with the sweat and swellings

of adolescence, dewy dumb
—the goosestep for fun?—
to its success in the formal
sense. See, no one has yet decided

much. Those horns-of-dilemmas
re: *you vs. them*
will soon be blown
until they're scarcely heard—
that's Vietnam. The band

puts out its collective foot
and wind bends itself
through brass arteries
and out the coned, plated

fronts of instruments, taking off
with a tattoo, with lunch's
doubledecker detritus flipping
in its wake, in the doubletime

that the majorette kicks to,
a *Whoopee,* let's march together at last
into the adult arms of death,
death, death until no one's left.

VETS

That ancient flag-carrying lot,
medal-chested with the defining deed of youth—
combat outside citizenry—with the *esprit de* corpse
of each for each, as gay as that, haunted
by when law goes absent and *to kill*
thrusts its imperative,

they prod the rest of us with weapon tips,
whet and sharpened still. Grizzled, even bearded,
feeble and en-wizened and perhaps
wiser than all the rest of us,
they march to quell youth—ours and theirs—
defining innocence, as vets do.

SLAVE CHILDREN

Qui tacet consentit
He who is silent agrees.

Something Latin here for
twelve hour days that says no play
but the fingers' equal
the tiny stitches of a bargain.

A soccer ball kicked—I'm not saying
it isn't my skin too. With days
for them a series of nights,
the idea of choice, just the idea—

not the way getting lunch early seems lucky—
is *Surprise!* They kill or work
as commerce requires,
necessity a little bracelet of sound.

A BAG, MOVING SLIGHTLY, IN BLACK AND WHITE

Inside—the head of a character, e.g. Death.

The weather map behind it says Okay in the states,
maybe it's a state that stares.

Simultaneous slide show—

animal out of an armature of rags,
no heads on portraits—

or Miss Wet, lascivious on another level or

just lips, still
over the abstracted liquid

from long pipes, drips only

down the back wall blank to torture,
where the gondolier's hat, what century?

glows, or a duck drowns. God forbid that bag—

I mean, that color
could be stain.

DETOQ

I know of no country in which there is so little independence of mind and real freedom of discussion as in America.

—ALEXIS DE TOCQUEVILLE 1831

Cars videotape the gun scene
with just the lens as witness,

the scrawl of the unseen
scrolling tic tic tic

through the machine.
Revenant is relevant:

a return from the dead,
a return from *Hello?*

electro-cardiogrammed.
There's no squirrel

in this. Freedom is not
atoms in envy. You feel

and report back and the atoms
pile up into pencils.

Even breath, the bread
in breadth chewed down,

our radiant future,
De Toq foresaw.

VOLKSSTURM

Boys, old men, anyone leftover,
armed at last with pots, good tin pots,
hoes with blades, clod-choppers
for dirt, forks sharp as nails,
fingernails. No action is what

they saw, just reaction: surrender,
the madmen's shouting turned
whisper, boys in tears. They
marched, big-bellied from
so few rations, legs barely lifted,

then they stopped. The victorious
proved too few, the MPs needed
elsewhere to guard paintings
like the ones my mother-in-law
fenced in the Sixties.

The old diplomat leans into my face,
says they shot them. *You didn't hear
about that, did you? Three hundred.
All they wanted was to go home.
Not a fork lost.* He makes to shove it.

HAMLET HIRSUTE

Who goes there? Hamlet
hirsute, furred as an old pickle,
dragging the skull as toy.

His chest hair waves:
To be or not? or *Tis nobler—*
whatever. Check the curtain.

Spy vs. spy vs. spy—
we're community, all healthy
curiosity. Ophelia doesn't sleep,

she circles her bowl,
eyes alert to all sides,
I's everywhere.

When nine of the elect
stand on chairs, we ask:
How high are those chairs?

They grow so old whispering
their lips whisker,
their tongues shake.

If we didn't have ears—
Instead they say
How soon can we sit?

AN OLD WAR

We mass, so many of us old,
with the old confusions of sex
and swarm, thrust and sting.

But we're not wasps or bees.
Try meteors. *Mom!* you screech,
ducking head-under-arms.

Impotence is not in any animal's genes,
it has to be earned. Forget the rockets'
red glare you so dearly love

and tear down that bright banner blood.
We can't be moths attracted by light,
we must—*boy*—chew at the fuse.

VERY FORGETFUL

The Obamas' pre-inaugural visit

Lincoln lounges in his chair.
The clang and whoop of party din—

of actual people, not plastic politicians—
braced for by a guard

with a flashlight, lantern-type: *Hope.*
Obama and his girls stand in the dark,

Booth in the shadows. *Carpe diem?*
The sun does rise again.

Washington's obelisk rises too,
billowing burnt fuel, virtually

starbound, the only firework.
We forget how the rational ennobles.

I THINK OF PILGRIMS

Frozen body discovered in undercarriage
of Air France aircraft July 2002. Also
2003 and 2005.

Not Cameroonians curled in the landing gear,
bound slaves of *isms,* to be picked off year
after year, homeland-torn and penni-
less for reasons of machete, too many
or too few. Everyone dreams of lolling
under fruit trees, Pilgrim breeches drying,
but such dreams mean money, highrise
-sized, where once the sun wouldn't rise.
Cellphoned to their continents, Pilgrims
from whatever persecution, kill those turkeys in
want, want, want, and the landing gear drops.

TRAINS IN THE DARK

Split from space, time-launched but time-less,
our car carries night itself. There's a through line

between apocalypse and shock, that word
coined when trains first carried man past beast.

We're post, the bomb's gone off a hundred times
a hundred, the soup of it invisible in our breath,

not even fog against the pane, this soup the train
drives into, end game. The post modern,

post feminist, post digital, post/pillar/post—the whistle's
already blown, we're shocked, sliding mercury-like

between rails in a soup of space uniting time and trouble:
Middle East, North Korea, *Oz* pinpricked into a balloon—

the posts we pass hold upturned boots,
the posts—those blurred flashes—all khaki.

II

YOUR AWFUL WEDDED HUSBAND

She translates this as *Man surpassing
all others in marriage.* Close,

says the native speaker, but no cigar.
She goes for Freud here,

20th century metaphor, the boxful.
Right, says the man. Encouraged,

she takes up her pen, kisses him, etc.
I know the word for this, he says. Wait.

Instead she bicycles
to a development lake to free

the fish from the market,
letting it swim off, newsprint

leaking ink into the water:
a man walks into a bra.

WHOSE XML

Dancing with code,
finger-licking digital
numbers letters symbols—
oh, *symboliste*, the hatch
marks, the amper-
sand but not its beach,
just the brick-and-mortar,
the clickables,
dancing out the terms
and conditions,

indivisibilities in the kitchen
of one-zero exactly,
each step tango or not,
knit one, knit No,
the algorithms
fast stepping, password-
protected but innocent of
elegance, cutting
and pasting without scissor
or sticky, the analogy

unhooking while
words rush unintelligibly
down an electric
river grokked and grokked

by froggy brackets.
How strange
your own elements,
too close to read. Robots—
those anaerobic nano-

bacteria lined up
on the thrush edge
of the wave, the bye-bye
of electron in your fingernail—
Limit says their screen or
flashes a connect sign
you don't know. As if
the Ladies is wanted,
no one signal gives you
an inkling,

the smallest ink of where,
Insert here. Smudge
purifies the corners
of this "earth," this series
of *Results,* the important
series half a parens later,
in which logic lies.
If x, then y.
Solve for sex.

SUSURRUS OF SHEETS, GOODBYE

He leans across his arm, peeks
at her hose-crotch bed-height,
her breasts doubling over.
It's no artist's pose, feet in a basin,
pin shivers in pointillesque,
but the hair she holds off her neck
sends heat into him. Otherwise,

color and motion, the day's
global positioning ratchets
into place with a purse click.
Sweet, she says into the near dark.
She could mean the sudden breeze
except he catches her hand
against his rough cheek.

APHRA PLAYS

Aphra Behn is not wearing all her clothes
in a part of South America nobody knows.
Everyone is polite, and not. Maybe she left off
her petticoats, her skirts look limp. She coughs.
Of course her bosom is bare. He's bats

about her, also noble and misunderstood—that's
too much culture for you. His black skin
is just skin, what with his wealth, *frisson,*
and all those bearers and banners.
The play is predominant, their manor-

house-reach. What she makes of it—not of husbands,
not even of the rights of humans richer-than-
thou, the local gentry who scheme more
than they breed—is insolence, not to bore
us. What is real is real, she says, wearing

what he wants with *Damn the insects biting.*
His type tends to the florid. Strange
how everyone speaks well of him, then how chains
become him—who says that?—and someone dies,
someone like her father who fuelled a nice

plantation with witty wives and loneliness and slaves
enough to drive the horses into pantaloons and full sleeves,
or play. Aphra grins at us, in disrepute
as always, sailing to England on a petticoat.

JEAN/JEANNE BARET

*"Baret carrying . . . even on those laborious
excursions, provisions, arms, and bulky
portfolios of specimens with a perseverance
and a strength which gained for him from
the naturalist the nick-name of his "beast
of burden."*

—*French Explorers in the
Pacific,* JOHN DUNMORE

I sailed high seas and low—
so plate-flat and hot the fish that flew
dropped and beat the deck.
        Then I sunned,
though circumspect,
           one pale limb at a time.
No one noticed what linked them:
        this middle with none of a man's business.
        I used a horn to make the proper arch with my water.

        Five months. Halfway around.
I'd be the first. As inflated in their genius
        as in the contents of their pants, all under
                Bougainville
        did not guess
save the plant man who gave me
        salves to poultice a pregnancy,
        and the thickest books
        to bear across coral under noon suns.

Thus when the boils on my hand
burst, one of the males (by the plumage of the island)
laid a flower on it

      and sniffed my neck—

                    he knew.

Just the books
      banked against me kept him
           from entering me.
           I made my voice go deeper,
I danced on his feet. I ran.

      Alone on a spit a mile further.
I recalled how these islands roast and eat white women
      if there's a question of whose:
           easier to divide.

Rabbit-still,
      I stared at the ship, lagoon bound, bobbing.

      That night the sailors peeled
a coconut crab and found it red with egg

               and ate it.
      I watered the plants.

      On rumor, Bougainville himself
sent a man.
      We are loathe to err, he said.
The crew, from bosun down, laughed,
           then feared,

a woman on board, and all that. I got the brig.

Then two of the natives ate our mirrors
and their deaths made my sex
of less interest.

In weeks, syphilis showed itself

especially among those who did it,
as is the custom, in the open, in dance or song,
     the maidens, they said, forcing them,
         showing their *Ta-hee-tees.*

They would call out for their salves—Jean, Jeanne.
                       We sailed.

No more sun shone for me
     until the specimen they took wanted a white
        woman.
Then I saw the sun—
     and ate rats after, chewing the tails down,
     my *merci.*

                Bougainville said I'd be famous,
first woman around the world, and he
the first Frenchman. He made it sound like marriage,
     not history.
Then he stopped the boat.
Here's an island, he said, for you and the botanist.

                But I made it back.
                The footnotes read:

She sailed for Madagascar
and married a planter.

       Planter? A few years on Marseille's dock
     strutting, rouged, with my mother,
and the future lifted—forget history.
It's all plunder for me and my pirate
partner.
            There'll be a beard soon enough.

STEAM SEAMS

Today's white plume of steam
becomes Miss Success d'Estime
in a nightie
if you look and look away
into the queue of satay-
loving coupon-holding tourists
expelling their reviews of bream
baked a la Manet.

Tomorrow's plume might be dream-
proof, a caterwauled ghee
of electrons in play by Faraday
you breathe in
only once, Saladin-
suspect, no believer.

Make hay
as if the meme
of chance has fled with your nightie
and left your wrists
tied and your fingers dream-
ing, while the teapot gleams.

OCTOPUS

After cueing, he stretches TV height,
runs a couple of Fahrenheit-
hot-hormoned, tricep-bicep-and-vein-bulging
arms your ass-wise, while in
full sostenuto, lays out each syllable
of your name. Then all his pockets fill.

You eye the beer he bought you,
even lean in to watch him voodoo
the geometry, the physics, the smack
of cue-to-green, fingers sliding off-rack,
the sudden weight of his thumbs hooked
to your jean belt, his cigarette sucked

so his *Hi* heats your ear, the way his hand
arcs around to powder the tip damned,
destined to drop to your nipple,
waist, crotch as if will
is nothing you can accuse him of, glancing
shark-like at a green ball, the scene

so early on your rights-radar you sip
at the beer, you lean back to gossip
with the ham-thighed matron handing out nuts
(his?) who might be married to him. *Buttercup?*
he calls her, *Hit me again.* And for once
she does, educationally, a straight-on punch.

RENDEZVOUS

In the glen of my heart,
where baton-white tails of Dear
scare, in this clearing that I snowshoe
into, in serious sweat, tripping on twigs,

maybe by a half moon or full
enough I see the forest open up,
these stuck-in-the-snow trunks
pretending to their rows, an evenness

that this heart 'o mine envies, breast-
beaten and stupid half the time,
the other half lost, *where did we
put it—love? It can't be far,*

I just set it down, where the creepy owl
sweeps past, and I expect
a cackle, not a *Who?*
where the tracks, so bare in the fresh

fallen fluff lead out, thank god,
made by the one who introduced us,
Miss Serendipity, who's gone to Florida
but has left us suet. You

will be furry and sleepy
after I clear the clearing, *bête
noire, nette bois, fête* Rene Char,
the fire insta-light between us,

its ash filled with messages
about what happened there.
Anyone who can read them
will surely lay the logs again.

BICOASTAL

Him in the sun is not fun.
Every day of mine is a white bit
of kleenex, with not enough air

to float. Our son asks:
Is he back or forth? I say:
Dream him here.

A fog descends after his takeoff.
How much is memory? Twenty cents
he's left on the bureau.

A month of cold phones, only food
children eat. My held breath is all
I'm counting up to.

Let the continent flex its bicep,
a man built on steroids. Absence
spreads—there's nothing like presence.

TWO GROUNDHOGS

Surely no man is carrying off your sheep?
—ODYSSEUS

Nobody's entrails lay out like hair.
Two groundhogs dance the polka
around that hair, smelling high summer
wet down by sweat.

I'm not watching, I'm stroking hair
on a chest as broad as a Louis in Philadelphia
or a John in Memphis, I'm stroking and laughing
in a harp way, a glissando all the way to groundhog

heaven, which is not Nobody's.
High, so high. Sony-like, sunny
and lonely together, like the charge of money
touching a place it shouldn't.

He took the heaven right outta me.
Bent hook of pity! The hogs I lay
tail to lip, connect up not pity
but war—that laugh again, high,

the biting of another's rear.
I shave and truss them, dead-hungry,
sure hogs make pork.
Pigs! The chest I abandon

heaves out *her,* the end of
Sweet Slaughter, myself
in the near future. Curse that Louis!
Review the entrails instead of hair,

believe in those true groundhogs
who polka for Nobody, the wood
soon dark and the dance so short,
where *Merci* won't mean mercy.

HURRICANE GIRL

She outlines her eyes with ink
from a Bic. In war or ardor?
The ferry's bow light

misses her head's *No.*
The wind gathers, two boys
mount awful cries

for parents lost to luck,
a handsome reflection pulls
waterside with damaged goods.

Now you can almost read her face,
so blue-scrawled the others
turn on her, a rising roar.

✖

Girl, girl, girl—sentries cliffside
lean out. Rain-wild,
they wave, spare hand on hem,
It's safe here. Safe.

Men slide the deck, barely glance.
Soon no girls but one—

she hoists her skirt.
A trick, screams the captain.

To the men who scavenge,
she worked and went home.
To the girls who wring out her hair,
she widowed herself.

✖

A ladder runged with knives
to the top, the locks blown

at the door, then the step out
into air. Too much victory—

outline the v twice.
I'm sorry. I am sorry.

A flag over her body.
Doesn't she look nice?

Guinevere slept with x
who slept with y.

Sutures sound like futures—hers?
A tiny cat, fake fur still attached,

the switch missing.

ANIMAL LOVER

A horse rises in a balloon
full of writing.

You could ride it yourself
and get no farther than brother,

the animal inside clawing out.
You are an animal

though you seldom achieve
such grace, except in cars.

The animal that directs your dying
Over here! with the wilder cells

bunches in familial nests
very close to *I said that.*

But birds still fly as birds.
They blue themselves with sky

up-side-down in your iris,
the brain a penguin turning one egg

with its toes in such cold.
When the animals call out:

Human! Human!
you shout back:

I am nude enough.

III

MISS GIVINGS

Livid, the blue infant she forgets in the sink,
slid so far on his side she thinks
he's about to prove she's truly jinxed.

But right him amid the mixed drinks
and he writhes, he rails, he pinks
up nicely, dolphin-color, an unlashed blink.

MOM AS FLY

A fly with a human head
heads for your screen. It's Mom,
toting groceries and laundry,

way too tiny. An interruption in scoring.
But first, score a bill worth
the trouble. *Mom! A twenty?*

The fly mounts the monitor
and notes the debt to education
remains unpaid.

But past midnight, theorems
are not her thing. Way faux,
as in eternal, those problems.

She handrubs. You crush her,
forgetting anguish might lead to food.
No buzz to you equals a faster connection,

where all relationships worship
the math, holy Pythagorean. But you
don't have the millions of eyes

she had to watch over something.
What was that something?
Your hand drifts to a pimple.

Could it be?
Dad decks you bad,
the triangle so over.

STALLED

The boy sees Man coming up soon. He stalls.
You hold the gate open, you curry. You google

the weather, hie sandwiches. The analysts are all a Go.
The significance of you magnifies, fault and catalyst,

tit and boot. You can do no wrong, no right.
The mystery is love, not fear. The horse loves you so much.

No. The unconscious loves itself, preservation,
the Latinate for *life,* must be invoked in this stall,

this *je refuse,* as autistic as that. Not the three-year-old's
sudden loss of words but a skewed wariness,

possible probable repetition of fear, a kind of death.
Man arrives anyway, strides out of the perspective,

the trap set for us all. *You could be wrong about that too,*
he says. *The horse let itself out.*

CARWRECK

> *They command us, though they speak no words.*
>   —SOPHOCLES

So Sophoclean, Mother on her Day beside the phone.
Not the cell. No—no *beside* with cells.

The framing is rather ugly, says Monopoly.
Instead, a fructose chirp from the fake cherry,

a billowing car part after halting.
This picture's all we've got.

Hydrangea blanches and looks less posh—
the framing mocks Mom like hotels

no one stops at with rude stuff left poolside.
A bird enters and you can't believe

how the door that frames the sign with the word
printed so small from here, how it was left open.

Mother on her Day takes the car apart
rather than frames it, the parts plant-entwined,

just needing dirt. Monopoly won the fake
two hundred dollars just by showing up,

no cell alert, and by reading the small print—
bird track really—beside the fuel

pooling in pink and green slick.
Mom! The very word.

LOVE LIGHT

The tomato sauce upsets twice,
almost suffocating his small self,

that much sauce—but no blood,
no, the dream's resistant,

not a single lip's
bitten for the taste.

Certainly I taste
the silky wave of sauce

and inhale and cough
then wipe his face with my skirt

that could be skin the way
I pull it from my hips.

I have to undress him, the groceries
cold in their cans,

the red pouring out meaning,
canceling light so close

you groan, almost
inside me. I open

my eyes, the curtain glowing
across the alley

as red
as flame.

Grief
can be that strong.

FLAW

a fortiori Stanley Plumly

It is because happiness
requires a flaw, as in beauty,
to make it perfect

that the inversion
of dead child to parent
turns the vase so perfectly.

Beauty beats him against her,
his death as fresh
as the rose inside.

Happiness has no god,
just wonder. How she wonders
at this beauty,

how it mimes
birth, her only template
for loss.

BURNT HOUSE

Leave the rest to the gods.

—HORACE

He tells his mother to go to bed.
I'll smoke, she whines,
not a day all alone

in her life. He's left his book
at the station, fifteen years
of names and numbers.

Leave, she says, *leave me
like an adolescent.* Something
from Horace here, not too

consoling. While he's out,
he doesn't hear the sirens. No one says
she's the same. His mother loved

her legs. *They seem to have grafted you
more,* he says. She raises
her lush, singed brows to his face.

Smell this, she says.
*It's age and yourself that consumed me.
The fire was mine.*

MY MATURE STYLE

I light matches endlessly.
Paris burns!
The Eiffel Tower shoots blue gas!
The lighter I find in my pocket—

cold metal on a blue bruise—
ignites the biggest fires.
I get dogs and cats running,
I get affirmation in black.

My mother's heart keeps on burning.
Mark the left ventricle her favorite,
its system so silent and skilled,
its blue the blues of exchange.

WOMAN WITH NAVEL SHOWING

Flat out *No* is all that fills
her body: she admires
those people who stop

their hearts. She lies abed,
growing hair and nails for her coffin,
doing nothing. Suicide is nothing

special, good reason gets ahead of
so much effort every day.
Have mercy! We outstretch our arms.

Mom, a palindrome
soon enough on stone.
In the fairy tale she grows

fur and claws, and tries to eat us.
In nomine matri.
Sweet, sweet, she says, caramel foaming.

She's not even hungry.
Tomorrow we'll throw open the doors
and invite everyone to the screening,

every frame forgiveness
but with subtitles too light to read.
You, we, I—it's all too intimate.

Let us be them.
Let them address you.
The iron in irony rusts if I weep.

A WOMAN LOVES HER BEATER

In amongst the branches with nothing better,
she operates her churn, her veritable spoon-
a-matic, her chainsaw deluxe on whatever
male or minor or charlatan animal.

Or mineral. The vegetables, clutch-of-wild-berries
hunted and gathered by her digits frozen off or almost,
are foraged from the deeply frozen. The branches
do part, as in death do us. A white Pyrex bowl,

deeply sided, consoles her, shiny on its raised dias,
the kind a politician or an undertaker would go for.
She climbs in to flee the dark forest's broken or beaten,
to cream, *tempo allegro,* Dante Alighieri.

THE GIFT OF FUNNY

For geographers Kath and Julie

Funny gift: the palate click,
the native wit, the grit of place
wherein the phrase pronounced just so

takes the brain pronto to
some outer island of stiff wind
that shoves every vocal effort

back in, into that brain's
primus start. What is an ear
but half the joke? Two girls, ga-ga,

who knows what sets them off—
Clean underwear crossing the road?
so wild they fall to the ground

where they walk, writhe along
the white line, *A dirty joke?*
rolling as if they could get it off,

Can't breathe it's so bad, so bad
they don't hear Mother's car,
their faces twisting, cresting again

and again, exquisite, *What did you say?*
Mother driving so far so fast,
with real Hell to pay.

DAD IN SUSPENDERS

The apples he picks
hold stars inside—cut one way—

and stars as pseudo as Mars
hang in the sky we lie flat enough

to be pierced by,
gazing, while Dad plans to crisp

those apples to tempt
Mom who weighs zero,

confused by models we didn't know
she knew, and apples

fall all around him,
hitting him—with a clot

in his head that could kill him.
As he pares,

he talks of details that make his life
dream—that red, from where?

and chuckles, some would say
desperately, expelling bad air,

the tears in his eyes
not from onions. Who's listening?

Apples roll all around him
like the stars we watch that fall

not so far away, while he plans
cutting the tree down,

hating trees, view-hoggers,
water-guzzlers. *You could be*

Martian, we phone to tell him.
Hardly any trees there.

That would make you what? he says.
Light's just boughs somebody's cut.

DAD AUBADE

Worry, a kind of aubade
where the lover, mornings,
doesn't leave, she's dressed,
her shoes are tied but.

I stretch my face Dad-
like, Dad's in my huff
and sit-up puff. Why
worry? He's only dizzy.

I shower it off. All night
I've hammered doors shut
with my heel—I'm going
to do better tight-chested?

I telephone and *love*
is what I tell him, and he
laughs like it's a lie and says
It's too early to call.

PINEAL

Such a gland manufactures sadness
in, say, white gobs

that creep from where
the third eye has sunk to,

unable to bear evolution's
blind trajectory.

Arrowing back on a plane
to where I lived before

the diaspora of highway, ambition
gassing my escape, I sense

the gland is old-teenaged,
menopausal, sick with theatrical sob.

All these extra people
rowed beside me had parents

and forgot them, except for a few
portraits. How to worship

that state I am soaring toward,
the state of the body,

its father,
its mother.

DICK IS DEAD

1930–2002

Dick is dead.
Paedophelia has lost its head.
Long live the town instead.

Photo and radio pro,
he issued invites and bon mots
to wives waiting by the telephone

while bedside,
awash in *au jus,* kids cried.
He didn't catch AIDS.

He did
the annual ski trip
with skinny dips.

No-Knock Dick,
he invaded our house with lilacs
or booze or new paint chips.

Only one
of my brothers broke down.
We are glad Dick is gone.

APPREHEND US

Creepy, the way the building bows.
It's not about wind.

I hold my sister's hand.
Time travels:

here we salute the weatherman,
and all those dead people

we both can't forget.
If you get into trouble, I say to her.

She hisses: *Remember the dodo.*
I say dull gulls

of people do things
to each other too. She says

turn left for the sadists
who make no cry,

right for the screamers,
mouths dark with opening.

It's just directions, I say.
But I swallow.

One man so careful
in speech his mouth twists

with *Why not,*
invokes a Greek god

famous for his sexual eraser.
His light is left on, he lights our walk.

TO MY BROTHER, ON THE OCCASION OF HIS SECOND BREAKDOWN

—after Dylan Thomas

In such darkness you're not listening:
bees, corn and tumescence
take up space, silence the landscape.
The hour of your seeming quiet
soon passes, plowed under.

If I trouble your sinking so much
you see the bottom
and the matching silences of moth,
money and the worm, am I a prophet,
is it foretold, the deft seed
whirling from a height?

The fury and majesty of a mind's death
I can't watch enough of
to keep you from teasing it closer,
your innocence springing clear too far
to be of any use but in blasphemy,
what you fall into

in such silence. You are deep inside,
I believe, beaded with tears.
If dollars wave in the fields, blood floods them
until the dark pollinates and must be cut.
The winnowed take a stiff drink, Lethe's.
After this first death, there is no other.

ANOTHER BROTHER

He keeps looking at that window,
      shut still, but he keeps touching the glass
where a spidery crack almost opens it. He keeps
         tapping it there and sometimes I see him press the seams
            where the putty's gone, just to feel it sharp.

He's not looking out, but in,
      the other side is as opaque as a mirror, nothing
         nothing nothing. What birds see? He bumps it,
knocks himself to sleep sometimes,
sometimes his head hurts.

      Seated, his hands lie level with the ledge. A plant
could tendril its way in, the window is open so long.
            He takes seasons
      to find its weeping light.

         I think the pane reflects his shine, the polish
         that comes to people who keep looking.
               Could wind
         be whistling against it? He doesn't say.
His hands lift to the sill, in greeting.

HAND QUEST

Tonight in your dreams you must look at your hands.

—CARLOS CASTANEDA

You have to put it up
      in front of your face
           in your dream.
I can't, I'm asleep.

Nevertheless you have to,
to see yourself.
It must be your own hand,
yourself
      in the palm's mirror.
Before you sleep say,
        I have to put it up.

Oh, my god, my god!
You can fall down before it,
but the hand will fall too.
               Put it
in front of you whenever

you face front.
The palm says *Hi, this is a dream
you are in.*
      The hand opens your eyes.
Everyone wakes here.

IV

WOOLY BULLY

Matty told Hatty about a thing she saw.
—SAM THE SHAM AND THE PHARAOHS

Something is too late,
her walk, her look?
Those in the know know

she could fix it with effort,
the transparent lie.
She could walk further

but she leans away from the path,
she stops to check the time.
How do you change it?

Her spouse tries out
an answer. There,
in the air, rushing

toward them at a fixed
rate, comes the sound of a sound—
watch it now, watch it.

THREE PLUCKED LADIES

Three plucked ladies chemo-
glutted, cocktail-wavy,
radiate into my kitchen.

Oh, my. Food is beside itself,
dust balls. You've seen
curtains hang?

Even the little threads
fighting the chair
retract when they sit.

But words waft,
heads hum,
bulbs on.

An offering of *me,*
as generous as that, there is
no other. I want to pray

but it's too late, they've harked
in semaphores, in series,
in sighs a whole meal of

Good Gracious. I hug them well,
their thin selves. I tuck each into
her trauma. I turn my head.

ALVEOLI

Could be birds on branches
clicking their hot-tailed haunches

against bark your ear can't avoid
comparing to your under-deployed

lung's catch in the middle
of every exhale while its liquid bubbles

higher, the yellow casualties winning
the war, pus filling

to ear-level. Lying flat tips the vial
beyond breath, the airline style

U-pillow alone keeping you steep
enough, it's only pneumonia, not sleep.

Could be bird's wings stuck in the shell,
could be a klaxon's *Very well*.

SELF INTEREST

No one says *No.*
The blue hairs of the race Otherwise,
the professors penciling Thanks,
enter and look—

the Exit. They say nothing.
Self interest, not fear, mutes.
A nice sound on a trumpet but
Hey, we're not practicing.

Is this the ebb, is this flow?
These weeds of a gene a fly tends,
these weeds are Us. What about *No?*
Just as we fathom *Now,* which fork

when or how to *Thanks, no thanks,*
they elongate their necks to check
what they can say—exactly.
You know then they never will.

THE WIDOW'S WALK

Memory in widow's weeds,
with naked feet.

—AUBREY DE VERE

The widow walks on glass.
You can see her panties
if you monkey under
or her beating heart
like a muskrat's or a toad's.
She carries it tucked
though ravens lower talons to it.

Or gulls, for water creeps
and clots, waves and washes
the sandy periphery.
The widow jumps from
the glass, her waist
at twenty inches nipped
by whalebone or the glass,

she jumps headlong and longer
through our viewfinder
trained on iron pickets,
wind sylvan through her hair.
The glass cracks, artsy cracks,
the hourglass of her
whipping with the rhythms

of the fire in the chimney
you want to pour her into.
Instead, ravens beak
through the shards
where she struts still,
either a miracle
or a TV episode that's final.

HALF GRAPEFRUIT

The knife reveals the world stopped
in a fruit, its eerie imperfection due
perhaps to physics, or more sun

here or there, or—
                        Grand design
frowns, taking account. Nothing suggests
doom will look different,

all asymmetry or so skewed you frighten,
you weep astringent. What can you tell
the child, his spoon so paused?

You stare into its slick face so long
you stare into self, surely.
You don't squeeze it.

MUSK AND MUSKMELON

The lake stood and pudding-
shook, the sails slack and dry.

Two men sang wholly songs—
no oaths—then drank a toast to me.

Tra-la. Their feet went pit-a-pat,
the engine turned and turned. Musk-

melon gained on the big big board
with big big money down.

The two (one to do the cover up,
one to prise the lid) checked out

the light they thought
the melons' night might lift.

The lake stood taut as taffy stood
the boat another drink. Then

musk turned slick as baby's spit
with stink who would have thought.

So take it out or drown it—
the feet went pit-a-pat. My own.

BAD NEIGHBOR

All the ivy ever cannot
cover what you see
in peekaboo. The great fly-by-nights,
Satan and his fold,

hoot in fabled swoops
announcing what you glimpse
as more of a problem than them,
ex-mammals cruising
tonight's skies.

Out of you, like an electric alarm,
a chirp dits its way into
Hello. Science says nothing's lost,
then it hedges.
The hedges, as square
as the capital letters important
books begin with, screen

the neighbor but not
his feet—could shoes do,
the part for whole, each
for Each?

You'd rather find
a length of snake or hose
about to strike,
not one bad neighbor.

THE DOG IN THE WALL

They said that's where Lulu
went, that was the smell. Not
rats.

Fifty years go by. They say
Yes, they don't change their story,
it's true.

A low cement-block fence around
the house, a collie dog bark,
four kids.

Not collie but collie dog, Howdy
as in Doody, The Stooges on someone else's
TV.

It barked less than we kids
howled, all of us waiting to move in,
the dog's tail

in our faces. No room for a big dead dog,
our first built house,
2 by 4s

at most, no crawlspace. Propitiatory,
an offering to a worksite in winter,
a shovel

to the head? They laugh.
We never saw the dog again,
the old house

too far to run back to, our scent long gone,
the busy roads with their big cars,
the pawing,

clawing against the sheetrock
my ear touches. Squirrels? The panting.
The whine.

MIDWEST GLACIER

They could not tell a plow from a pumpkin
—from *The British in Iowa,*
JACOB VAN DER ZEE, 1922

No pop left in the Kool-
pop, just ice and dust,
a surprising climate
said the exiled lord
in Iowa, generations before
the dust bowled. Now his great-great's
truck's snout coughs climate-
change, one
that sucks,
no matter what flavor the Kool-pop, how much
dust there is
to disappear in.

I clear my throat,
a dramatic sound that disturbs
the gods here; motes flash.
To get anywhere,
I must appease,
offer salve,
pet the burnt orange and sooty

cows. They gasp, the ones not roasted
or poisoned, carrion-proof

      for they have swallowed the dust.
The problem devolves
to the animals, splayed belly-first
      in the hopeless state,
the pride of.
I'm thinking *who what*
where like a journalist,
      I'm still trying to see the glacier
a-glitter, saved.

CYCLES

For Amy Tan

Without a moon or light,
my bike floats, all balance.

I open my mouth, *O sole mio*
but my voice could be the road,
dippy and suddenly ending.

A friend bikes out of the black.
I heard you and I hurried.

I wobble, startled, but my wheels
whine forward. We can't even see
the grass brushing our calves.

Soon the road narrows
and a creek cuts one side,

you can hear water
on its own path, and surely
there's a ditch—surely.

We bike in file, hunched,
bearing the dark until

a car comes up behind us,
lights off. We pedal hard, harder.
The car comes on anyway,

it is coming. Before its grille heat
signals where,

there's a terrible crash,
the late pop
of an airbag, there's the ditch

and the grass, we weave and—
There's no sound after,

just a metal something
rolling,
We kickstand our bikes.

No *O my god.* Just *What?*
What? my friend, gasping.

We run back.
If we search for the driver apart,
we're lost, but together,

we're doubly blind.
We touch and touch.

The sharp grass, the flitter of insects,
the uneven earth underfoot—
we want not to find

anything. But Death says
we must, both of us,

and the road
we followed, the road
the car left,

will disappear.